Did You Ever Wonder about
Things You Find at the Beach?

written and illustrated by Vera Vullo Capogna

BENCHMARK BOOKS

MARSHALL CAVENDISH

NEW YORK

Benchmark Books
Marshall Cavendish Corporation
99 White Plains Road
Tarrytown, New York 10591-9001

Library of Congress Cataloging-in-Publication Data
Capogna, Vera Vullo
Did you ever wonder about things you find at the beach? / Vera Vullo Capogna.
p.   cm. — (Did you ever wonder?)
Includes index.
Summary: Describes various kinds of sea creatures, shells, and other objects which can
be found on the beach especially after a low tide.
ISBN 0-7614-0851-7
1. Seashore biology—Juvenile literature. 2. Seashore—Juvenile literature.
3. Beachcombing—Juvenile literature. [1. Beaches. 2. Seashore.
3. Seashore biology.] I. Title. II. Series.
QH95.7.V85   577.69'9—dc21   97-47119   CIP   AC

Printed in Hong Kong
1 3 5 6 4 2

To my parents, who gave me the opportunity to explore beaches as a child.
And to my husband—only through his confidence and support was this book possible.

With thanks, too, to James A. Ebert, wildlife biologist at the Fire Island
National Seashore, Long Island, New York, for his generous assistance.

The beach is full of wonders.

Have you ever just sat at the shoreline and watched the waves curl up along the sand? Did you ever wonder what causes these waves? Or what makes the water rise up on the beach? Or where the sand that you build a sand castle with comes from?

Did you ever wonder about all the interesting things that you find while walking along the shore?

This book will explain all you may have ever wondered about while at the beach.

If you scoop up a handful of sand and look at it closely, you will see that it is made up of tiny rocks.

Sand begins to form as wind and water rub against the earth's surface. Large rocks wear down and pieces of rock get washed down rivers and streams. As these pieces flow downstream, they rub against one another. They become smaller and rounded. This is how sand is formed.

When the sand in the rivers reaches the sea, it is tossed about by the waves. The sand finally washes up on the beaches.

While at the beach you may have noticed how sometimes the water covers a big part of the sand. At other times the water goes back down, leaving the sand uncovered. This is the changing of the tides.

Tides are caused mainly by the moon pulling on the earth. The ground under the ocean stays still and only the water moves. During high tide the water moves slowly toward the land. During low tide the water moves away from the land.

High tide

There are two high tides and two low tides each day.
During low tide, as the water moves away, it leaves behind shells, rocks, and seaweed. Sometimes it leaves small animals stranded. This is a good time to go looking for signs of sea creatures and for finding shells and other interesting things.

Low tide

Have you ever found something at
the beach that looks like this?

This is called a mermaid's purse.
You may be surprised to learn that
it is an egg case of a fish called a skate.
Skates lay their eggs in pouches like this
for protection. After the eggs are hatched,
the empty black cases wash ashore.

It's exciting to find a sand dollar at the beach.

Sand dollars are flat round animals. They bury themselves in the sand at the bottom of the ocean and plow along searching for food specks.

When a sand dollar is alive, it is brown or purple. The white sand dollars found on the beach are really empty skeletons. They have been turned white by the sun.

A live sand dollar

You probably know what a starfish looks like. But did you ever wonder how a starfish sees? Or how it eats? Did you know that if one of the arms of a starfish is broken off, a new one will grow back in its place?

If you turn a starfish upside down, you will see its mouth. Since a starfish has no teeth, this is how it eats:

First it grabs its prey, which might be a clam or a mussel. With its feet acting like suction cups, the starfish slowly pulls apart the two halves of the shell. The starfish then pushes its own stomach through its mouth, eats the meat, and finally, pulls its stomach back in!

This small round disk is the breathing organ. It lets water and oxygen flow inside the starfish.

Turn a starfish over and you will see its mouth and feet. Its feet act like tiny suction cups that help the starfish grab the ground or rocks as it moves around.

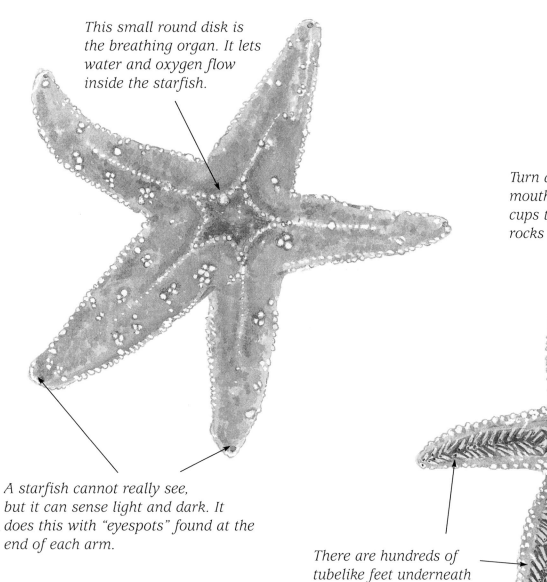

mouth

A starfish cannot really see, but it can sense light and dark. It does this with "eyespots" found at the end of each arm.

There are hundreds of tubelike feet underneath the starfish's body.

While walking on the beach at the shoreline, you might see tiny hills that look like this:

These little hills are made by the lugworm. Next to each hill is a small hole. Beneath the hole is a tunnel where the lugworm lives.

The worm sucks water and sand down into its hole. It eats the tiny pieces of food found in the sand. But the lugworm cannot digest the sand. So it passes the sand through its tail and out of the tunnel. This is how it makes these spaghetti-like hills.

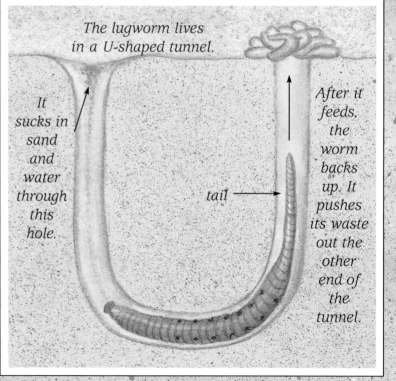

The lugworm lives in a U-shaped tunnel.

It sucks in sand and water through this hole.

tail

After it feeds, the worm backs up. It pushes its waste out the other end of the tunnel.

The lugworm repeats this motion all day long.

Have you ever seen blobs of clear jelly lying on the beach? These blobs are actually dead jellyfish. Waves sometimes wash jellyfish up on the beach. They cannot live out of water. Slowly, the air and the sun cause them to shrink. After a while they turn into small blobs of jelly.

Jellyfish *do* sting, but they *do not* attack. The sting occurs when the tentacles of the jellyfish touch your skin. It feels something like a tingling shock.

SEA NETTLE

MOON JELLYFISH

If you ever find a jellyfish that has been washed ashore, don't touch it. Even out of the water, the stinging cells keep their power for some time!

tentacles

We all enjoy swimming in the water at the beach or feeling a wave curl up and tickle our toes. But have you ever stopped to think about where these waves come from? Or why the water looks blue and tastes salty?

The salt comes from rocks on land that the sea covered many years ago. Salt is still entering our oceans from rainwater. Rainwater dissolves the salt found in rocks in the ground. Rivers then carry the salty rainwater out to the sea.

Although the ocean water appears blue, it really is clear. The blue is just a reflection of the blue sky. On a cloudy day the ocean appears a dull gray color.

Waves are caused by wind. Wind blowing over the water surface causes tiny waves. The stronger the wind blows, the higher the waves. The waves grow bigger and bigger the longer the wind keeps blowing.

While walking along the beach, you may have stopped to pick up some seaweeds. Seaweeds are plants that grow in water. Instead of roots, they have holdfasts. These help the plants cling to rocks.

There are many kinds of seaweeds. They can be found in different shapes, sizes, and colors.

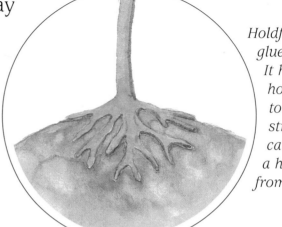

Holdfasts have a gluelike coating. It helps them hold on tightly to rocks. Even strong waves cannot tear a holdfast from a rock.

Pieces of oarweed are sometimes broken off by waves and washed ashore.

TOOTHED
WRACK

OARWEED

The edges of toothed wrack look like the edges of a saw. That is why the plant is sometimes called saw wrack.

SEA LETTUCE

*Some fish lay their eggs
in seaweed such
as this thong.*

THONG

Did you ever wonder why
seaweed is so slimy? Many seaweeds
live underwater close to the shore.
When the tide runs low, they are
uncovered. Their slimy coating
prevents them from drying out in
the sun and air.

*Many people have fun popping the
little "balloons," or bladders,
found on bladder wrack.*

*Dulse is a pretty
red seaweed.*

BLADDER WRACK

DULSE

Have you ever stopped to pick up a shell at the beach? Shell collecting is lots of fun. Many people forget that empty shells were once the homes of living animals called mollusks.

Since mollusks do not have any bones, their bodies are soft. Their hard shells protect them from enemies. Mollusks are attached to their shells and live in them. When the animal inside dies, its shell is washed ashore.

WHELK

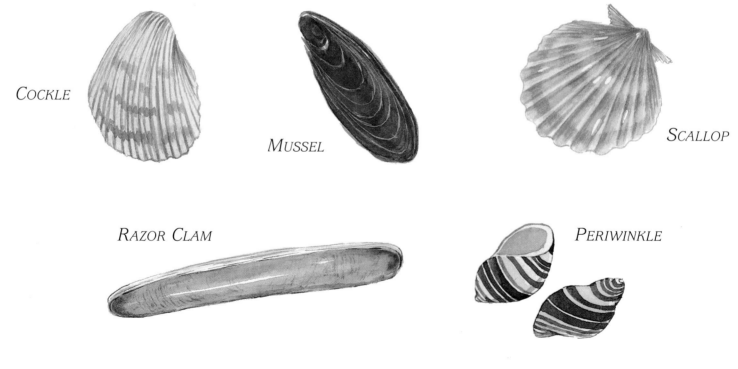

COCKLE

MUSSEL

SCALLOP

RAZOR CLAM

PERIWINKLE

These are some of the most common shells you might find at the beach.

Hole made by moon snail

Have you ever come across shells with little round holes in them? Did you ever wonder how those neat little holes got there?

The holes are the work of certain sea snails that feed on other shellfish. One such snail is called a moon snail. The moon snail first uses its large "foot" to grab its prey. Then it takes its very rough tongue and drills a hole through the animal's shell. It sucks out the meat through the hole and eats it. The empty shell with the hole in it is then washed ashore.

MOON SNAIL

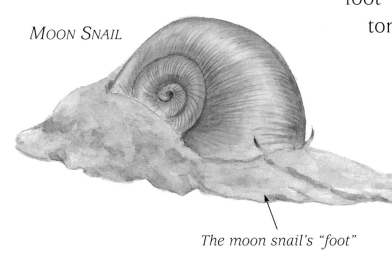
The moon snail's "foot"

Sand dunes can be found on almost every beach. They are found in the dry part of the beach that is farthest away from the water.

Dunes are formed as the wind blows dry sand. The sand stops when it hits plants that are growing on the beach. Little hills of sand form around the plant roots. The more the wind blows, the bigger the dunes get.

Many wild animals such as rabbits, raccoons, and even some crabs make their home in the dunes.

Plants such as this beach grass help hold sand dunes together.

Ghost crabs live in sand dunes.

A visit to the beach is never complete without meeting a crab or two.

One of the strangest-looking crabs is the male fiddler crab. He has one enormous claw and one small claw. The fiddler crab's large claw is brightly colored. He uses it to attract the attention of female crabs. He shakes the claw up and down and from side to side. This also scares away other male crabs.

When the fiddler crab waves his big claw, he resembles a person playing a fiddle. That is how the crab was named.

If you ever see a fiddler crab shaking his claw at you, beware! He's not waving hello!

Another interesting crab you are almost sure
to see is the horseshoe crab. Its empty shell can
often be found at low tide.

A horseshoe crab is not really a crab. It is
actually a relative of the spider. It got its name
because its shell is shaped like a horse's hoof.

Many people are frightened of this creature.
Its huge hard shell and long pointy tail look
very scary to some. But a horseshoe crab
is really harmless. It spends most of
its time plowing through sand and
mud searching for food. It has
four eyes but can only see
blurry shapes. So it must
use its sense of smell to
search for food.

tail

eye

eyes

eye

You can easily spot a horseshoe crab's trail in the sand. It has three paths. The two outside paths are made by the shell. The path in the middle is made by the dragging tail.

Certain crabs called hermit crabs
do not have shells of their own.
These crabs use the empty
shells of other animals
for their houses.

A hermit crab
hardly ever leaves
its shell, not even
to eat. Only when it
outgrows its shell does
the hermit crab leave it,
in search of a larger one.

*Hermit crab living inside an
empty shell*

The seashore is home to many different kinds of birds. At the beach you'll find birds that eat crabs, fish, and other small sea life.

Seagulls like the beach because they can find food such as dead fish or garbage that people have left behind. Seagulls have sharp bills shaped like spears. They use them for stabbing fish and other food.

Sometimes gulls make pests of themselves. They gather around beach blankets, waiting for any scraps of food they can snatch.

HERRING GULL

COMMON TERN

Terns look similar to seagulls except they are a little smaller and have pointier bills. Most terns have black on the top of their head and neck.

It's fun to watch terns as they dive headfirst into the water for fish.

Sandpipers are amusing to watch as they seem to be racing the waves.

The sandpiper is a bird you will find often, mostly at low tide. Sandpipers have long legs and long bills. They use their long bills to dig up worms, snails, and other tiny creatures. Their long legs keep their bodies above water as the waves wash ashore.

You probably have seen groups of these birds running together. The waves seem to chase them up the beach. When the waves roll back down, the sandpipers follow. They're looking for tiny shellfish that may have washed up with the waves.

This is a sanderling, a member of the sandpiper family.

If you've ever picked up a piece of damp seaweed, most likely you've noticed tiny bugs jumping about. These are sand hoppers.

Actually, sand hoppers are not bugs at all. These small creatures are relatives of crabs and lobsters.

Sand hoppers hop along the beach searching for food. They eat seaweed and tiny animals hidden among grains of sand. As they hop along, they leave behind a trail of dents in the sand. These tiny animals sometimes hop as high as twelve inches!

Although sand hoppers are sometimes called beach fleas, they don't bite like dog fleas might.

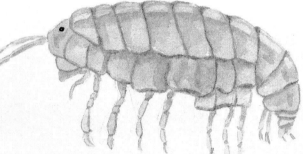

SAND HOPPER
(three times its real size)

Sand hoppers can be found at the high tide line eating washed-up seaweed.

Have you ever found a large rock with many little cone-shaped shells attached to it? These shells are actually barnacles.

At first glance barnacles don't appear to be living things. A barnacle comes to life, however, whenever a wave washes over it. Tiny threads appear from the top of each barnacle. These threads are its legs. When a barnacle feeds, it sticks out its legs and kicks tiny pieces of food into its mouth!

When young, barnacles attach themselves to a rock or other large object. They stay in the same spot their whole lives. Some barnacles even attach themselves to whales and sea turtles. They travel with them wherever they go.

Feathery legs of a barnacle feeding

There are always so many interesting things to discover on a trip to the beach.

GLOSSARY AND INDEX

BARNACLE 29
A small sea animal with a hard cone-shaped shell. It lives its whole life attached to a large object such as a rock.

DUNES 22
Hills of sand along the beach. Dunes are formed by the wind. Grasses and plants usually grow among them.

FIDDLER CRAB 23
A crab with one claw much larger than the other.

HERMIT CRAB 25
A crab that doesn't have a shell of its own. It uses the empty shell of a mollusk for its home.

HOLDFAST 18
The bottom part of a seaweed that holds the plant tightly to a rock.

HORSESHOE CRAB 24
A crablike animal with a shell shaped like a horseshoe.

LUGWORM 14
A worm that lives in a tunnel in wet sand.

MERMAID'S PURSE 10
A small case in which certain fish lay their eggs.

MOLLUSK 20
An animal with a soft body, no bones, and a hard shell to protect it. Mollusks usually live in water.

MOON SNAIL 21
A mollusk named for its round whitish shell. The moon snail lives in the sea and eats other mollusks.

PREY 12, 21
An animal that is hunted by another animal for food.

SAND DOLLAR 11
A round sea animal that lives in the sand at the bottom of the ocean. Dead sand dollars are white and can be found washed up on many beaches.

SAND HOPPER 28
A small animal, about one inch long, that is related to shrimps and lobsters. It hops along the beach looking for food.

STARFISH 12, 13
Not a fish at all, but a flat animal, shaped like a star.

TENTACLES 15
The long skinny arms of some animals such as jellyfish. The tentacles on some jellyfish sting when touched.

TIDE 8, 9, 19, 24, 27, 28
The rising and falling of the ocean. Tides are caused mainly by the pull of the moon on the earth.

About the Author

Vera Vullo Capogna is a freelance writer and illustrator with a bachelor's degree in fine arts from the School of Visual Arts in New York City.

Inspired by her love of nature and the outdoors, she decided to write a series of nature-related books for children. Many of the topics covered in her books are in response to things her own children have wondered about.

Born and raised on Long Island, New York, Vera loves to explore its many beautiful beaches with her husband and three children.